Coyote Ridge Elementary School
13770 Broadlands Drive
Broomfield, CO 80020
720-872-5780

MW00604017

A Civil War Drummer Boy

The Diary of
William Bircher
1861-1865

Edited by Shelley Swanson Sateren,
foreword by Suzanne L. Bunkers

Content Consultant:
Hampton Smith, Reference Archivist,
Minnesota Historical Society

Blue Earth Books

an imprint of Capstone Press
Mankato, Minnesota

Blue Earth Books are published by Capstone Press
151 Good Counsel Drive, P.O. Box 669, Mankato, Minnesota 56002
http://www.capstone-press.com

Library of Congress Cataloging-in-Publication Data
Bircher, William, 1845-1917.
   A Civil War drummer boy : the diary of William Bircher, 1861-1865 / edited by Shelley
Swanson Sateren; foreword by Suzanne L. Bunkers.
       p. cm. — (Diaries, letters, and memoirs)
   Includes bibliographical references and index.
   Summary: Excerpts from the diary of William Bircher, a fifteen-year-old Minnesotan who was
a drummer during the Civil War. Supplemented by sidebars, activities, and a timeline of the era.
     ISBN 0-7368-0348-3
     1. Bircher, William, 1845-1917 Diaries Juvenile literature. 2. United States. Army. Minnesota
Infantry Regiment, 2nd (1861-1865) Biography Juvenile literature. 3. United States—History—
Civil War, 1861-1865 Personal narratives Juvenile literature. 4. Minnesota—History—Civil War,
1861-1865 Personal narratives Juvenile literature. 5. United States—History—Civil War, 1861-
1865—Participation, Juvenile literature. 6. Boys—Minnesota—Saint Paul Region Diaries Juvenile
literature. [1. Bircher, William, 1845-1917. 2. United States—History Civil War, 1861-1865
Personal narratives. 3. Diaries.] I. Sateren, Shelley Swanson. II. Title. III. Series.
     E601.B605 2000
     973.7'81—dc21   99-28816
                                                                              CIP

Editorial credits

Editor: Chuck Miller

Designer: Heather Kindseth

Photo researchers: Kimberly Danger and
   Heidi Schoof

Artistic effects: Louise Sturm-McLaughlin

Photo credits

Minnesota Historical Society, 6, 8, 27, 28;
Library of Congress, 7, 9, 10, 19, 20, 23,
24; Gregg Andersen, 11, 14, 16; Archive
Photos, 17, 21, 29 (bottom); North Wind
Picture Archives, 29 (top)

CONTENTS

Editor's Note

The Diaries, Letters, and Memoirs series introduces real young people from different time periods in American history. Whenever possible, the diary entries in this book appear word for word as they were written in William Bircher's original diary. Because the diary appears in its original form, you will notice some misspellings and mistakes in grammar. To clarify the writer's meaning, corrections or explanations typed within a set of brackets sometimes follow the misspellings and mistakes.

This book contains only portions of William Bircher's diary.

William's entire diary spans almost five years and is much longer. Text sometimes has been removed from the individual diary entries. In these cases, you will notice three dots in a row, which are called ellipses. Ellipses show that words or sentences are missing from a text.

You can find a more complete version of William Bircher's diary in the book *A Drummer Boy's Diary: Comprising Four Years of Service with the Second Regiment Minnesota Veteran Volunteers, 1861 to 1865*. More information about this book is given in the To Learn More section on page 31.

FOREWORD

I started writing in a diary when I was 10 years old. At first, I wrote short entries about the weather, family activities, schoolwork, and friendships. I soon began to write about my thoughts and feelings. My hopes and dreams for the future eventually found their way into my diary. I have kept a diary for more than 35 years. Writing in it is still one of my favorite things to do.

Diaries like William Bircher's and mine are called primary sources. Primary sources are letters, photographs, diaries, and other materials that give firsthand accounts of people's lives. They detail the events and feelings people have experienced. We learn about personal views of history from primary sources.

Today, primary sources such as William Bircher's diary show us how people lived in the past. We learn about the challenges people have faced. We learn about their accomplishments. Their stories help us understand how past events have led to the present.

Suzanne L. Bunkers,
Professor of English and
Director of Honors Program,
Minnesota State University, Mankato

William Bircher
A CIVIL WAR DRUMMER BOY

William Bircher lived with his family on a farm near St. Paul, Minnesota, when the Northern states and the Southern states began fighting the Civil War (1861–1865). Like many other 15-year-olds, William was excited about the war. He wanted to become a soldier in the Union Army and help the United States defeat the Confederacy.

People in the South were concerned about the election of Abraham Lincoln as U.S. president. Lincoln and many people in Northern states such as Minnesota favored a strong national government. People in Southern states believed state governments should hold most of the power.

Northerners and Southerners also had different ways of life. Most people in the North owned small farms, ran businesses, or worked in factories. Officials in Northern states said they did not need slaves to help them earn money. They thought the national government should make slavery illegal in all states. People in the South owned small farms or ran large plantations. People in Southern states said they needed slaves to help grow and harvest crops. Southerners thought each state should make its own laws about slavery.

Officials in Southern states thought Lincoln would work to take away states'

William Bircher was at first rejected by the Union Army because he was too young to be a soldier. But Company K of the Minnesota regiment needed a drummer. William was allowed to join the army as a drummer boy.

About 620,000 Union and Confederate soldiers died from battle or disease during the Civil War. Many were buried in military cemeteries like this one in Alexandria, Virginia.

rights on issues such as slavery. Officials in Southern states believed their states should leave the Union. On December 12, 1860, South Carolina became the first state to secede from the Union. The other ten Confederate states quickly followed. On April 12, 1861, Confederate soldiers opened fire on Union troops who refused to leave Fort Sumter in Charleston, South Carolina. The Civil War had begun.

Minnesota Governor Alexander Ramsey visited Lincoln in Washington, D.C., to offer the president the services of the First Minnesota Regiment. On June 14, 1861, the regiment was ordered to Washington, D.C.

Minnesota officials soon began forming the Second Minnesota Regiment. William tried several times to join this regiment, but was turned away because of his age. Finally, in the late summer of 1861, William was allowed to enlist in the Second Minnesota Regiment as a drummer boy. His parents objected at first, but soon even William's father felt a patriotic duty. He enlisted in the regiment with his son and drove a supply wagon. William would not see his father much during the war, however. Supply wagons traveled back and forth between the supply lines and the battlefields.

Many of the three million Americans who fought in the Civil War were boys. Both the Union and the Confederacy required soldiers to be eighteen years old, but many boys lied about their age. Many other boys like William were allowed in as musicians.

The Civil War was the bloodiest war in all of North American history. About 620,000 men and boys lost their lives. Nearly 500,000 others lost a limb or suffered a painful wound.

William was lucky. His life was spared and he was not wounded. But William learned that war is not a fun adventure. In his diary, he wrote about the discomforts, sacrifices, dangers, and hard work of war.

The Diary of William Bircher

July-August, 1861—

. . . I had made several attempts to get into the regiment but, not being over fifteen years of age and small in size, was rejected. But Captain J. J. Noah, of Company K, seemed to think that I would make a drummer, as the company was in need of one. I was then taken to the office of mustering-officer Major Nelson and, after being questioned very carefully in regard to my age, was not accepted until I should get the consent of my parents . . .

. . . The happiest day of my life, I think, was when I donned my blue uniform and received my new drum. Now, at last, after so many efforts, I was really a full-fledged drummer and going South to do and die for my country if need be . . .

From 1861 to 1865, Fort Snelling in Minnesota was a training center for thousands of volunteers who joined the Union Army.

Regiment Bands

Each Civil War regiment had its own band. The bands practiced every day and often cheered the troops with concerts. Nearly 40,000 musicians served in the Union Army and about 20,000 served in the Confederate Army.

Drummers and buglers played especially important roles in the Civil War. Buglers played the song "Taps," the signal for bedtime. Drummers beat morning wake-up calls and the call to meals. They also provided beats for marching drills and for marches to battle sites.

Though musicians did not fight, drummers did serve on the battlefield. Drumbeats communicated orders to the soldiers, telling them when and how to move. In the thick smoke of gunfire, drumbeats helped soldiers locate their units. Hundreds of drummers were killed as they provided drumbeats in the direct line of enemy fire. Thousands more drummers were wounded in battle.

Members of the Second Minnesota Regiment trained at Fort Snelling before they headed south to confront the Confederate Army.

Most Union regiment bands wore Union Army uniforms. Some wore fancier dress gear than others.

William spent August and September at Fort Snelling in Minnesota preparing for battle. In October, his regiment received orders to travel to Washington, D.C., to join the Union Army. But first, the Second Minnesota Regiment passed through St. Paul, Minnesota's capital city, on October 14. William wrote about the experience:

October 14, 1861—

. . . We found the city ablaze with bunting and so wrought up with excitement that all thought of work had been given up for that day.

As we formed in line and marched down the main street towards the river, the sidewalks everywhere were crowded with people, with boys who wore red, white, and blue neckties, and boys who wore fatigue caps with girls who carried flags and girls who carried flowers with women who waved their handkerchiefs and old men who waved their walking sticks . . .

The Second Minnesota Regiment left St. Paul that day and traveled by steamboat, by train, and on foot to Pittsburgh, Pennsylvania. There, the Union Army gave the regiment new orders to spend the winter marching, drilling, and making camp in Kentucky.

January 15 [1862]—

. . . We made a long march, and at night found ourselves in the wild woods without food or shelter and a long distance in advance of our wagons. Our pickets were posted within two miles of the enemy. We had a heavy rain the night before, and it had rained at times as we marched . . .

William's regiment was ordered to the Battle of Mill Springs in Kentucky. Confederate troops had attacked the Tenth Indiana Regiment.

January 19—

In a few minutes our regiment was ordered on to the field of battle. We marched by the right flank, up the main road, then made a left oblique movement, then regimental front, and double-quick time until we met the Tenth Indiana. Falling back—they having run out of ammunition—our regiment charged up to a rail fence, and here occurred a hand-to-hand conflict: the rebels putting their guns though the fence from one side and our boys from the other. The smoke hung so close to the ground on account of the rain that it was impossible to see each other at times . . .

Sometime in mid-February, the Second Minnesota Regiment arrived at a large farm near Lebanon, Kentucky. The regiment asked for food and supplies from the farm's owner, Thomas Jonathan Jackson. But Jackson supported the Confederacy. He started shooting at the regiment from his front porch before being captured. William and the regiment helped themselves to Jackson's belongings.

February 1862—

. . . We found his smoke-house well filled with choice bacon and hams, and his cellars filled to overflowing with all kinds of vegetables and preserves, of which we helped ourselves to our hearts' content . . . With full stomachs . . . on the following day, we bid adieu to the Jackson farm, and felt as though we had punished him just half enough.

William's regiment traveled by steamboat to Tennessee. The regiment received orders to aid the Union Army at the Battle of Shiloh in Tennessee. William's regiment marched quickly but did not reach this battlefield until the day after the battle.

April 1862—

The battlefield was strewn with the wreck and carnage of war. Caissons, dismounted cannon, and dead artillery horses and their dead riders were piled up in heaps, and the warm sun caused a stench that was almost unbearable . . . No historian can ever depict the horrors of a battlefield . . . Squads of men scattered all over the field digging trenches, rolling the dead in, and covering them up with three or four inches of dirt, only to be washed off by the first rain, leaving the bones to be picked by the buzzards and crows. Such is the terror of war . . .

September 16—

We marched twenty-two miles. I had no shoes. I tore up my shirt to wrap around my bleeding feet, which were so sore I could not march without great pain.

Barefoot March

Soldiers wore out boots quickly on long marches. A soldier had to keep marching even if his boots fell to pieces. Union soldiers often were not issued the uniforms and boots they wore. They usually were given a clothing allowance of forty-two dollars a year. But this money would not buy uniforms or boots if a supply store was not nearby.

Confederate soldiers had smaller clothing allowances than Union soldiers. Confederate soldiers were poorly dressed and many did not have shoes. Barefoot soldiers still had to march and fight in battle. Those Confederate soldiers who did not have decent shoes and uniforms took them from the bodies of dead soldiers. Union soldiers took guns and clothing from dead soldiers as well.

September 17—

We marched twenty-one miles to Bowling Green [Kentucky]. The dust in the roads was four inches deep, and the clouds that arose were suffocating . . .

September 25—

Marched to the mouth of the salt river, where it empties into the Ohio [River]. Here we found the boys all barefooted, and no shoes to be had. My rags were worn out, and I had taken the pocket from my blouse and wrapped it around my feet; but as it was very thin stuff, I did not expect it would last over an hour or so . . . We were furnished with a bountiful supply of bacon, hard-tack, and coffee, and we ate as only half-famished men can . . .

October 1—

We marched from Louisville and encamped eight miles from Shepherdsville. The country was destitute of water. None was to be had except in pools and puddles along the road, which was very warm and putrid. Weather very hot and the roads dusty.

October 4—

. . . Found a puddle where we dipped it up with a spoon and strained it through our dirty, sweaty handkerchiefs.

In the fall and winter of 1862, William's regiment continued to march through Kentucky, Tennessee, Missouri, and Alabama. The regiment often fought with the Confederates they met.

December 25 [in Tennessee]—

Christmas: A gloomy one for us. We had for our dinner a bill of fare consisting of baked beans, coffee, hardtack, and sowbelly.

Hardtack

butter or margarine for
  greasing
paper towel for greasing
5 cups all-purpose flour
1 tablespoon baking powder
1 tablespoon salt
1⅔ cups water
baking sheet

large bowl
dry-ingredient measuring cups
measuring spoons
liquid measuring cup
wooden spoon
table knife
toothpick
pot holders
spatula

What You Do:

1. Preheat oven to 450°F (240°C).
2. In bowl, combine 5 cups flour, 1 tablespoon baking powder, 1 tablespoon salt, and water. Stir mixture with wooden spoon. Wash your hands, then squeeze the mixture with your fingers.
3. Place a large dab of butter or margarine on the paper towel and use it to grease the baking sheet. Flatten the dough with your hands to a ½-inch thickness on the baking sheet. Shape dough into large rectangle.
4. Use table knife to lightly trace lines into dough to divide it into squares 3 inches by 3 inches (8 centimeters by 8 centimeters).
5. Use toothpick to prick holes all the way through and across the entire surface of the dough.
6. Bake 25 minutes or until lightly browned.
7. Let cool 10 minutes. Remove baked hardtack from the baking sheet with a metal spatula.

Makes about 9 crackers.

WARNING: DO NOT eat hardtack without first dipping it into milk or hot chocolate. Dry hardtack may break your teeth.

[December] 27th—

Called out at reveille to stack arms on the color line. It rained all day, turning cold at night and remaining so.

December 30—

I was ordered to beat long roll at 1 A.M., and remained in position until 10 A.M., expecting a skirmish with the Johnnies. While standing in line the boys suffered a great deal from the cold . . .

January 1, 1863—

. . . Vandyke and I were the only ones left out of the eleven drummers that left Minnesota in '61 and, of course, we had to do the entire guard duty. While sitting in the guard-tent I figured up the miles we had marched in 1862, taken from a daily account I kept, as follows: January, 101 miles; February, 149; March, 52; April, 158; May, 36; June, 129, July, 39; August 101; September, 258; October, 343; November, 98; December, 29; total, 1493 miles for the year.

William spent the winter and summer of 1863 in Tennessee. During these months, his regiment drilled, marched, battled with the enemy, and endured camp life.

January 8 [1863]—

Rain, snow, and hail all together made it more interesting. Such weather as this knocked all the enthusiasm out of trying to be a hero, and most of us were about sick of the hero business.

Sunday, January 18—

Warm and pleasant. Inspection of arms. Quartermaster issued boots and drawers, and the balance of the day the boys wandered around the woods hunting rabbits and gathering walnuts.

March 4—

Skirmished all day. Captured sixty-two prisoners and three hundred [Confederate] horses and mules. Marched nine miles.

March 5—

Marched eighteen miles to Chapel Hill, and drove the rebels out of town. Marched back six miles and encamped on a low flat with plenty of good water and plenty of wood.

[April] 25th—

R. G. Rhoades, of Company E, took the leadership of the band, and practiced for the first time. I held the prominent position of snare-drummer.

Saturday, July 4—

My seventeenth birthday. A salute of one hundred guns was fired—not on account of my birthday—but the birth of the republic . . .

August 19—

Hot and sultry. Marched down the mountain sixteen miles into the Sequatchie valley, where we found plenty of peaches, apples, corn, and an abundance of clear, cool water, which we appreciated, as we had had no water since the morning before.

In September 1863, William's regiment fought in the Battle of Chickamauga in Georgia. On September 19, Confederate General Braxton Bragg ordered his army of 66,000 soldiers to attack Union General William S. Rosecrans's army near Chickamauga Creek. Rosecrans's troops numbered 58,000. The Union soldiers were forced to retreat the next day, but Bragg's army did not pursue them. Bragg's decision saved many Union soldiers' lives and allowed them to help defeat the Confederate Army at the Battle of Chattanooga that November.

September 19—

Hot and dusty. At daybreak, as we marched along, we saw troops falling into line on the right of the road. The artillery was unlimbered, the gunners stood to their guns, and everything had the appearance of a battle. We marched along the rear of the line until we reached the left wing of the army, where we piled up our knapsacks, formed in line, marched to the front, and deployed skirmishers. We advanced but a short distance in the woods, which was a pine forest, before we came upon the rebel skirmish-line. We heard on our right the heavy roll of

General George Thomas gave orders from horseback directly to his Union corps. For his bravery in the Battle of Chickamauga, Thomas became known by his men as "The Rock of Chickamauga."

musketry and the terrible thunder of the artillery and it came nearer and nearer, until in less time than it takes to describe it, we were engaged with Bragg's army. The terrible carnage continued at intervals all day. At night we heard, from all over the field, the cry of the wounded for water and help. The ambulance corps were doing all in their power to bring all the wounded into our lines. The night was cool, with a heavy frost, and the water was very scarce. We lay on our arms all night . . .

September 20—

The battle was renewed with terrible slaughter on both sides. Towards noon we heard that Chittenden's and McCook's corps, on our right, had been driven back, and all that was left on the field to hold in check the entire rebel army, was our corps,—[Union General George H.] Thomas' Fourteenth. We held the enemy back until evening, in spite of his desperate assaults, and after dark we retired to Rossville . . . Bragg's army was too tired and too sadly worsted to attempt to follow on the night of the 20th.

September 21st—

A few straggling shots were directed against our army at Rossville. Thomas felt that he could not hold his position there against the Confederate army. Orders were received at 6 P.M. on the 21st, and by seven o'clock the next morning our army was withdrawn, without opposition from the enemy. This ended the battle of Chickamauga . . .

September 22—

Our band was detailed to the hospital to assist the nurses in taking care of the wounded . . . The large business blocks on the main street [in Chattanooga, Tennessee] were used for hospital purposes. We succeeded in keeping the men of our regiment all together on one floor. They occupied five large rooms, and it was heartrending to see the poor fellows as they were brought in, shot and mangled in every possible way. Every few moments we had to take one out who had died, and put him in the dead house, where he would remain until there was a wagonload . . .

William remained at the hospital until September 25, when he was ordered to return to the regiment. During his absence, the men had been building breastworks to protect themselves from the enemy's artillery fire.

October—

From the 20th to the 30th we did nothing but picket and guard duty . . . I was suffering with dysentery and found that most of the men were in the same condition. We had no bread of any description for three days.

In November 1863, William's regiment and other Union troops fought in the Battle of Chattanooga in Tennessee. Union General Joseph Hooker's troops captured Lookout Mountain while Union General Thomas's troops stormed Missionary Ridge.

Tuesday, November 24—

. . . We could plainly see General Hooker's troops charging up the side of Lookout Mountain. The heavy clouds, which all day had enveloped the mountain's summit and thus to some extent favored Hooker's movements, had

Death from Disease

Disease killed more soldiers than bullets did during the Civil War. Of the 620,000 soldiers who lost their lives, about 390,000 of them died of sickness and disease.

Men and horses living close together produced a great deal of filth. Garbage and horse manure littered the army camps. The soldiers rarely had enough water to bathe. Bacteria grew in these dirty conditions and infected camp food and drinking water.

William and the soldiers in his regiment often suffered from dysentery during the war. They ate spoiled food and drank dirty water, both of which caused this disease. The soldiers' symptoms included severe diarrhea. Many soldiers died of dysentery.

Antibiotics and vaccines were not available to cure deadly diseases in the 1860s, but many of the diseases could have been prevented. Clean food, water, and campsites for the troops would have meant fewer deaths.

Wounded soldiers were taken to field hospitals where they sometimes were cared for in tents or on the ground.

19

Union General George H. Thomas led Union troops, including the 2nd Minnesota Regiment, to victory at Missionary Ridge.

Union General Joseph Hooker led the Union troops that captured Lookout Mountain at the Battle of Chattanooga.

gradually settled into the valley, veiling it at times completely from view. Thus the battle of the afternoon was literally "a battle above the clouds." The enemy was repulsed, driven back from the last position where he could make a stand, and hurled over the rocky heights down the valley. By this time the darkness upon the mountain rendered farther progress extremely dangerous, and Hooker's troops encamped for the night on the slopes, which they so gallantly won. Lookout Mountain had been captured, and, before morning, the stars and stripes waved from its peak. The enemy had abandoned his encampment, leaving behind him in the hurry of his flight all his camp and garrison equipage.

November 25 [Missionary Ridge]—

. . . From the position we occupied we could see every movement of the enemy in the first and second line of works, and they were watching every move we made. We stood in line patiently waiting for the signal to advance. We had not long to wait, however, for at 4:30 P.M., from a signal gun at Orchard Knob, the entire army moved as one man (our regiment as deployed covering the front of our brigade) towards the first line of works, which we soon reached, and drove the rebels out.

Before we reached the first line of works we crossed an open piece of ground, and, as we left our cover of trees and entered this piece of ground, the top of the ridge was one sheet of flame and smoke from the enemy's batteries, and the grape [cannon fire] tore up the ground around us. The troops being deployed as they were, there were very few casualties. After taking the first line of works, the troops followed the fleeing rebels up the ridge and charged over the second line of works. Here our regiment captured a rebel battery. After the capture of this line, we had but little fighting. The rebel army was routed and fled towards Taylor's Gap in great disorder. We bivouacked on the battlefield for the night and felt that, under General Grant, we had regained what we had lost under General Rosecrans . . .

General Hooker's forces defeated the Confederate troops led by General Braxton Bragg at the Battle of Lookout Mountain near Chattanooga, Tennessee.

William's regiment remained in Tennessee until the New Year.

December 1—

We had a grand review. Generals Grant, Thomas, Hunter, and Reynolds, and a score of brigadier generals were present. After the review Colonel Bishop had inspection of regiment. Everything but our clothing was inspected. It was getting to be a serious matter with us. We had not changed clothing for a month or more, and the men were getting filthy and were covered with vermin. We . . . had to remain in this condition until we had clothing issued to us; and when that would occur God only knew.

December 5—

Cold, rainy, and misty. We received a large mail, and of course some papers. We could lie in our tents, under the blankets, and read and pass the time. But we had no rest; the gray-backs [body lice] kept us moving . . .

December 25—

Christmas: but how dark, how cold and dreary. How dismal everything was in camp. The band boys had all re-enlisted except Wagner and I, and we now made up our minds not to remain out. The others had used every endeavor to coax us in, so we at last consented and were mustered in for another three years.

In January and February 1864, William's regiment returned to St. Paul, Minnesota, on brief leave. This break was a reward for the soldiers who had re-enlisted in the Union Army and were now called Veteran Volunteers.

January 24, 1864—

We arrived at St. Paul . . . and proceeded to the International Hotel, where we were furnished with an elegant dinner, a compliment we, having traveled all day in the cold, heartily appreciated. After dinner I proceeded home to surprise mother, and, as it was dark in the house, she must needs call for a lamp to look me over from head to foot, while she was saying to herself, "God bless you, my boy!" Although I knew that my name had not been forgotten in the evening prayer all the while I was away, yet not once, perhaps, in all that time had mother's voice been so choked in utterance as now. With her heart overflowing, she gave thanks for my safe return. When I lay down that night in a clean white bed, for the first time in two and a half years, I thanked God for my safe arrival.

*The heavy artillery fire William
describes in his diary was caused by large cannons
like those manned by the Union soldiers in this photo.*

In March, William's regiment returned to Tennessee. They often fought in small skirmishes with the Confederates in Tennessee and Georgia during the spring, summer, and fall of 1864.

July 28—

> . . . The regiment was in splendid condition and were prepared to undertake and make a vigorous campaign against the enemy. On the 19th we marched twelve miles to the Chattahoochee river and encamped.

It rained most of the time, which kept the boys in their little shelter-tents. Immediately in front of our camp was the head-quarters of [Union] General Sherman, whom we saw at all hours of the day and night, marching back and forth in front of his tent, with his head bowed, chin on his breast, and his arms locked behind him. That night he made the rounds all night with the guard in front of his tent, occasionally stopping in front of the fire a moment to talk with him, then resuming his steady march. I had no doubt but that he was planning some campaign that would surprise the natives.

[November] 7th—

We made our first appearance with our new silver instruments and created quite a furor.

Union General William T. Sherman rested his troops in Atlanta before they burned the city and began the march to the sea.

On November 15, 1864, Union General William T. Sherman began a march through Georgia from Atlanta to Savannah. His Union soldiers burned bridges and tore up railroad tracks to destroy Confederate supply lines. The troops also burned Atlanta and much of the countryside. William's regiment was among the 62,000 men Sherman led.

November 15—

Weather cloudy, but warm and pleasant. Marched nine miles to Atlanta, and at night we destroyed the city by fire. A grand and awful spectacle it presented to the beholder . . . The heaven was one expanse of lurid fire; the air was filled with flying burning cinders . . .

November 25—

Left the city at 9 A.M. Burnt the bridge over the river at this place. Marched sixteen miles, crossing the Oconee River. We lost poor Simmers, the drummer of Company G, during the night. The poor fellow, being unable to keep up, lay down somewhere along the road, and was captured by the [Confederate] cavalry that were following us up. I took his blanket and drum to relieve him, but he was too fatigued to follow, saying, "Oh, let me rest. Let me sleep a short time. Then I will follow on." I tried to keep him under my eye, but he finally eluded me, and when we again stopped for a short rest he was not to be found. By that time he was most likely a prisoner. I pitied the poor fellow . . .

Union troops arrived in Savannah in December 1864 and camped there until late January 1865. In February, the Union troops left Georgia and marched into South Carolina. Many Union soldiers blamed South Carolina for leading the Confederate states in separating from the Union. Soldiers destroyed the homes, barns, and fences of South Carolina residents. William's regiment took part in this destruction.

[February] 16 [1865]—

Marched sixteen miles. Passed through Lexington Courthouse. The troops destroyed every house along the road.

February 17—

Cold and cloudy . . . The fences and buildings, the entire length of our day's march, were burning, and the smoke very nearly suffocated us . . .

Starting Your Own Diary

William kept his diary to record details about his life. He wrote about his experiences in the Civil War. His diary tells us about the lives of Union soldiers in the Second Minnesota Regiment. William did not know people would read his diary. He wrote it for himself.

You can keep a diary to record the details of your own life. You can write about the weather, family activities, school, and friendships. Diaries are a place to write openly about what you think and feel. You are writing for yourself.

People sometimes keep diaries all their lives. Diaries can become personal histories. Someday your diary might be a book like William's.

What You Need

Paper: Use a blank book, a diary with a lock, or a notebook. Choose your favorite.

Pen: Choose a special pen or use different pens. You might want to use different colors to match your different moods.

Private time: Some people write before they fall asleep. Others write when they wake up. Be sure you have time to put down your thoughts without interruptions.

What You Do

1. Begin each entry in your diary with the day and date. This step helps you remember when things happened. You can go back and read about what you did a week ago, a month ago, or a year ago.
2. Write about anything that interests you. Write about what you did today. Describe people you saw, what you studied, and songs you heard.
3. Write about your feelings. Describe what makes you happy or sad. Give your opinions about things you see, hear, or read.
4. Write in your diary regularly.

On April 27, William's regiment prepared for another battle. But soon after sunrise, an officer on a white horse appeared and cried out, "Peace is declared!" William's regiment immediately set out for Washington, D.C., and marched in the grand review on Pennsylvania Avenue. Then they traveled homeward by rail. Some men were bound north, some east, some west, but all were bound for "Home, sweet Home!"

July 20—

> We were then disbanded and said the last "good-bye" to our comrades in arms . . . Songs were sung, hands were shaken, or rather rung, many a loud hearty "God bless you, old fellow!" resounded, and many were the toasts and the healths that were drunk before the men parted for good.

William and the rest of the Second Minnesota Regiment's Band posed for this group photo after the Civil War ended.

Afterword

After the war, William remained in St. Paul, Minnesota. He ran a saloon called Billy Bircher's Place. He married in 1869 and had three children. In the 1870s, William became a grocer and began to hold positions in local government. William retired in Florida, where he served as mayor of the town of St. Cloud. He died on February 5, 1917, and was buried in St. Paul.

Timeline

December 12– South Carolina is the first state to secede from the Union.

April– The Civil War begins when the Confederates attack Union-held Fort Sumter in South Carolina.

President Abraham Lincoln declares the Emancipation Proclamation. This order said that all slaves in the United States were free.

1860　　　　　**1861**　　　　　**1863**

July– William enlists in the Second Minnesota Regiment as a drummer.

December– William re-enlists in the Union Army and is mustered in for another three years.

The Confederacy surrenders. The Civil War ends.

| 1864 | 1865 | 1917 |

November– William's regiment is among Sherman's troops who capture Atlanta, Georgia, and later destroy the city by fire.

February 5– William dies. He is buried in St. Paul, Minnesota.

Words to Know

adieu (AH-doo)—the French word for good-bye

ammunition (am-yuh-NISH-uhn)—things that can be fired from weapons, such as bullets or arrows

bunting (BUHN-ting)—small flags joined by a string and used for decoration

carnage (KAR-nij)—the killing of a great number of people, as in battle

drawers (DRORS)—underwear

gray-back (GRA-bak)—body lice

hardtack (HARD-tak)—a hard cracker

picket (PIK-it)—a detached group of soldiers guarding the troops against surprise attack

putrid (PYOO-trid)—decaying or rotten

quartermaster (KWOR-tur-MASS-tur)—an army officer who provides clothing for the troops

regiment (REJ-uh-muhnt)—a military unit

smokehouse (SMOKE-houss)—a building where meat is preserved by curing it in thick smoke

sowbelly (SOW-bel-ee)—salt pork and bacon taken from the sides of a hog

suffocate (SUHF-uh-kate)—to cut off the supply of air or oxygen

Internet Sites

American Civil War Homepage
http://sunsite.utk.edu/civil-war

Civil War in Miniature
http://Civilwarmini.com

Battle of Gettysburg
http://www.gettysbg.com/battle.html

Historic Fort Snelling
http://www.mnhs.org/places/sites/hfs

To Learn More

Bircher, William. *A Drummer Boy's Diary: Comprising Four Years of Service with the Second Regiment Minnesota Veteran Volunteers, 1861 to 1865.* St. Cloud, Minn.: North Star Press, 1995.

Dosier, Susan. *Civil War Cooking: The Union.* Exploring History through Simple Recipes. Mankato, Minn.: Blue Earth Books, 2000.

Hazen, Walter A. *Everyday Life: The Civil War.* Don Mills, Ontario: Addison Wesley Longman, 1998.

King, David C. *Civil War Days: Discover the Past with Exciting Projects, Games, Activities, and Recipes.* New York: Wiley, John & Sons, 1999.

Places to Write and Visit

Chickamauga and Chattanooga National
    Military Park
Superintendent
3370 LaFayette Road
Fort Oglethorpe, GA 30742

Gettysburg National Military Park
Superintendent
97 Taneytown Road
Gettysburg, PA 17325

Historic Fort Snelling
Fort Snelling History Center
St. Paul, MN 55111

Lincoln Boyhood National Memorial
P.O. Box 1816
Lincoln City, IN 47552

INDEX